Many Names

A book of prayers

by Yvonne Aburrow

Contents

Introduction

There are many different types of prayer. Many people think of prayer as "asking God to give us things". Most people rightly dismiss this sort of prayer as irrational and unspiritual. It's well known that the rain falls on the just and the unjust alike. Many people in the First World War prayed for their loved ones to come back unharmed, but many young men were killed, and I am sure their families prayed just as hard for them to come back as the families of those who returned safely. The First World War (and subsequent genocides such as the Holocaust) ended many people's faith in a personal God. This lack of a personal God obviously affects what we mean by prayer. When there is no person that we are talking to, prayer becomes a communing with the All.

At Unitarian Summer School in Great Hucklow, I attended a workshop about prayer with Vernon Marshall, a Unitarian minister. He identified many different types of prayer: adoration, devotion, prayer of approach, invocation (asking the Divine to be present), bidding prayer, confession and penitence, words of reassurance, thanksgiving, intercession (asking for help for someone else), petition (asking for help for yourself), healing prayer, expressing aspiration, and reflection. There are also specific types of prayer for different bits of the service – blessing the elements of communion, for instance, or giving the closing blessing.

Prayer can also be simple and traditional. When his disciples asked him how to pray, Jesus gave them a simplified version of the traditional Hebrew Kaddish prayer, which today we know as the *Lord's Prayer* or the *Prayer of Jesus*. This prayer contains hidden depths: it expresses many deep desires of the human heart – to be forgiven, to be loved, to be understood and to be nourished; and it expresses something about the nature of the Divine.

Informal and personal prayer is also valid; we tend to use written prayers in chapel, rather than extemporizing, but that is the nature of liturgical worship. There's nothing wrong with informal prayer in private.

There are also different modes and techniques of prayer: centering prayer, contemplative prayer, and body prayer (using dance or other special movements in prayer). These are the ones I am developing in my personal spiritual practice, because I want to live in my whole body and not just in my head.

But what is prayer for? I don't think it is really for God's benefit (though She probably likes to be taken notice of). I think it is for our benefit. The practice of mindfulness, of cultivating awareness of the greater life of the universe, and of examining our own conscience, and being aware of the suffering and joy of others – these are beneficial for the soul. St Paul said, "In him we live, move and have our being" and "we are all members of each other": we are part of the greater life of the universe.

In the Wiccan text *The Charge of the Goddess*, Doreen Valiente wrote,

"Arise and come unto me. For I am the soul of Nature, who gives life to the Universe. From me, all things proceed and unto me all things must return; and before my face, beloved of Gods and men, let thine innermost divine self be enfolded in the rapture of the infinite."

To "be enfolded in the rapture of the infinite" expresses very well for me what prayer should be like.

Charles Williams, a Christian mystic who was also a member of the Hermetic Order of the Golden Dawn, believed that God is in everything and everything is in God, and that we are all part of each other. If this is true, then it has profound consequences for prayer, because when you pray, you are connecting with the entire cosmos and all beings within it, and so the healing of your own soul is also the healing of all other souls.

Mother Theresa was once asked about her prayer life, and she said that she didn't talk to God, she just listened. The interviewer asked her what God did, and she replied "He just listens too." Silent prayer and contemplation is probably the most powerful form of communication with the Divine, because we spend so much time focused on words that we lose touch with the more instinctual side of our nature.

Contemplative prayer is an age-old tradition of mystics. It is quite similar to centering prayer, but doesn't involve a specific concept; it's more of a wordless communion with the Divine. It is usually preceded by more verbal forms of prayer, which lead into contemplation or meditation.

In Kabbalah, the mystical tradition of Judaism, there are four worlds or stages of creation, and when we pray, we ascend through these worlds to come closer to God; they also correspond to psychological states. The closest world to the Divine Source is Emanation (Proximity in Hebrew); the next is Creation, then Formation, then Action. The soul in prayer ascends through the worlds of action (the body), formation (the ego), creation (the soul) and emanation (the Divine presence).

In Eastern Orthodox Christianity, there is a tradition called Hesychasm. Hagia Hesychia or Holy Silence is an aspect of Christ, and Hesychasm is the practice of silent prayer. In some ways it is similar to Quaker practice (which is interesting when you consider that there is no historical connection between them). Holy Silence is traditionally represented as female, and there is a lovely icon of her by William Hart McNicholls.

Staretz Silouan, a monk of Mt Athos, recommended praying for everyone you know and just holding them in your awareness and love. Similarly, a Buddhist meditation of *Metta Bhavana* (loving kindness) invites you to love yourself, then your partner, then your community, then someone you dislike, then the whole world.

Centering prayer was developed by an interfaith dialogue group of Christians and Buddhists. These Christians admired the technique of Buddhist meditation but didn't want to cultivate the awareness of the Void recommended by Buddhist tradition; so instead they decided to choose a single concept and focus on it during the meditation, which they called "centering prayer". So for instance you might choose the word "Love", or "Peace" or "Joy" to focus on during the prayer. The technique is similar to that of meditation, in that you relax your breathing and focus on the body, but you hold the concept you wish to focus on in your heart for the duration of the prayer, perhaps repeating the chosen word. We tried this earlier.

Body prayer is where you involve your whole body in the act of prayer. This might be gardening and praying, or dancing and praying, or walking and praying. Walking a labyrinth can be a prayerful act, as you deliberately focus on the spiritual journey. Another example of body prayer is the Dances of Universal Peace, a dance tradition in their own right, designed to engender peace and love in the participants; another example is the Salute to the Sun found in Yoga (which is a sacred Hindu practice designed to stimulate spiritual growth); yet another example is the Muslim style of prayer, which was also used by many Christians in the Middle East (indeed in some places, Christians and

Muslims used to pray side by side). Similarly, Taizé prayer is an ecstatic form of prayer involving the whole body.

So prayer can begin with words, and end with silent contemplation. There are many different kinds of prayer, using words, gestures, dance, and silence. All are beneficial to the spiritual practitioner, and to those around them, as they cultivate peace.

The other day a Catholic friend posted on his blog that Christian mysticism is more interested in the practice of compassion than in achieving rarefied spiritual states. This is probably true of all the world's great mystical traditions; but I commented that the two approaches go hand in hand – you cannot practice compassion unless you are also at peace with yourself; and you cannot be at peace with yourself unless you practice compassion. You cannot separate the inner work from the outer work, because your inner state and the outer world are intimately connected. As D T Suzuki once said, "Our ego is just a swinging door between our outer and inner world." And, I would add, it is prayer that opens the door between the two worlds.

Prayers to the source

Mother Goddess

Sinking gratefully back into the land,
Into the folds of the Mother,
Her creases in time and reality,
Her magic is a wrinkled apple,
A golden ball dropped from a tree's galaxy of branches
into Her green and fertile lap
where it will decay and then grow into a tree.

O Mother I hear your call,
the wild clear call of the Moon,
the barren and compassionate one
who gazes down upon the Earth,
your green and blue sister.

May I dance with the Sun, Moon and stars;
May I feel their dance within me
and know that it is the One at play in the many -
the dance of being and non-being,
the laughter and tears of the divine at play
in each one of us -
wearing different masks,
now tragic, now comic.

May I hear the song of the stars,
feel the rhythms of the Earth pulse in my body,
lie upon the beloved land
and know that my depths are Her depths
all the way to the ends of the Universe.

17-10-2011, 11.35 am

Mother Spirit

God our Mother: the source and origin of all life
Who is in both the starry heavens and the fruitful Earth
We sing to you of your beauty,
And we cry to you when we are in pain,
We whisper your many names into the night.
Your presence is everywhere
Your song is the music of creation, perpetually renewing itself,
Reflected in the patterns of Nature and the movements of the stars.
You feed us from the bounty of Nature's store
And nurture us when we are in pain,
When we have hurt others,
And give us the strength to heal and forgive.
May we not harm the delicate web of existence,
But help to heal and strengthen it.
For yours is the beauty, present in everything,
The ever-changing beauty of Nature,
Throughout all existence
Amen.

16-1-2011

Prayer of Yeshua

O Genderless Engenderer,
Flame of life at the heart of all things,
Holy, holy, holy are your names.
Your republic of informed hearts is always within us and around us.
Your mysterious way unfolds before us
as matter and spirit dance together to create life.
May the finite tell its stories to the infinite
and may the infinite lend its everlasting peace to the finite.
May our hearts be open to forgiveness given and received,
and may we move accurately in harmony with all
and remain present in the now.
The republic of heaven on earth is all and each of us
reverberating with glory and power
in infinite space-time.
Amen.

26-8-2009

A prayer inspired by the Tao Te Ching

O Source of all being,
Name unnamed,
You are the pattern of the flight of birds,
You are the silence behind the wind,
You are the wave and the water.
We do not know the pattern,
We do not listen to the silence,
We do not see the water, only the waves.
You are the Great Mother:
empty yet inexhaustible,
giving birth to infinite worlds.
You are always present within us.
May we know the way of the universe,
May we find the pattern,
May we hear the silence,
May we be like water,
Flowing in harmony with the All.
Amen.

Source of all beauty

O Source of All Beauty
May we see the beauty in the humble and unexpected:
      the patient spider and the wayside flower,
      the daisy and the buttercup;
      the wheeling of silver birds against a leaden sky.
May we manifest the sacred art of love
      in all our words and deeds,
      and forgive ourselves and begin again when we fail.
May we tread gently on the Earth
      who is our holy Mother
      and protect her from harm.
May we honour the sacred in the everyday:
      a smile, a look, a word; a simple act of kindness;
      a meal shared, or help with mending.
Amen.

Source of all life and love

Source of all life and love,
Divine presence in our hearts and in the world
Ground of our being,
Source of wisdom and compassion,
We come to you in silence and stillness
to hear the beating of the mighty heart of the universe.
The way of silence opens our hearts to compassion;
The experience of awe and wonder leads our minds to wisdom.
Let the head and the heart be united in the works of our hands
as we labour to build a world where justice and peace may flourish.
Let us cultivate the virtues of tolerance, acceptance and inclusivity,
Let us celebrate freedom and diversity, thought and contemplation,
Let us devote ourselves to the quest for truth
that can only be revealed by reasoning about experience.
Let us honour all those who have worked for freedom of conscience
Enabling us to live in the beloved community we share
And to show forth in our lives the golden heresy of truth.
Let justice roll down like waters
and righteousness like an ever-flowing stream.
Amen.

A communion prayer

Loving source of all existence,
As we eat and drink together,
    we partake of the great communion of all life,
    and are reminded of our common source.
We have renewed today our covenant of love
    with each other,
    with all beings,
    and with the magnificent universe that is our home,
    and the source of our existence.
May we share our blessings with all whom we meet.
Amen.

This day
I desire to make connections
  to sustain a sense of the sacred
  to be graceful and gracious
  to listen to the silences between the words
  to be mindful of the beauty in each moment
  to give thanks for the beauties
    of tree and flower,
    birdsong and laughter,
    friendship and fellowship.

Great Mystery at the heart of all that is,
may I be constantly aware of the wonder and joy
of being awake, alive and aware
and treasure each moment
whatever it brings

and when I fail,
as often happens,
let me not be too hard on myself,
but gently reconnect with the heart of the mystery
sinking gratefully into the soft darkness,
the singing silence.
For each moment we can begin again.
It is never too late.
The time is always now.

23-6-11
7.55am

From the rising of the sun

Praise be to the source of all life.
Praise, all beings who come from the source, praise the source of all life.
Blessed be the source of all life from this time forth and for evermore.
From the rising of the sun until its setting, praise the Name that cannot be named.
The source transcends nations and boundaries, and its glory is beyond the heavens.
Who is like unto the source of life, which dwells in the deep,
The source that becomes like the earth
  to behold the things that are in heaven, and in the earth!
The spirit of life raises the poor out of the dust, and lifts the needy out of the dunghill;
And sets them with princes, even with the princes of their people.
The life wells up even in the barren, and makes them joyfully bring forth life.
Praise the source of all life.

(A NeoPlatonist / Taoist / Unitarian version of Psalm 113)

Prayer for liberation

O deep and ineffable Silence
That speaks from the depths
O space carved out by suffering
That is inexplicably filled with joy
You are the inspiration of our going forth
To connect with others
Move our hearts to compassion
That we may genuinely lift up the poor
Move our hands to action
That we may lift the burdens of the oppressed
Fill our heads with inspiration
That we may behold the vision of a just society
And work to bring it into being
Amen.

22-7-2010
(inspired by liberation theology)

Prayers of life experience

Sunshine after rain

Light unending
Light transforming
Light revealing.

The world is transformed by light
especially after rain.

The rain makes everything seem grey and misty
But it washes the dust and weariness away
And when the sun returns,
everything gleams, fresh and bright,
colours sparkling.

The light renews the world,
transforms it,
reveals its brilliance.

Water and light: sources of life,
refreshment and renewal.

The soul's seasons are like this:
tears and laughter, water and light.

When the tears come,
may they be swiftly followed by laughter,
Laughter that renews and refreshes,
illuminates everything
and reveals the joy,
the inexpressible joy
at the heart of everything.
Amen.

19-6-2011

Sleep

Where does the mind go during sleep?
Does it rest in the Divine?
Wherever it goes, it returns refreshed
from the shores of forgetfulness.

And what of dreams,
those messengers from the deep?
Beautiful and fearful,
they bring up treasures and horrors
from beneath the sea.

My body sinks thankfully into sleep
like a sloth settling onto a branch.

Let us be grateful
for the gift of sleep
and the healing it brings.

Let us be grateful
for the gift of dreams
and the insights they bring.

1.30 pm
8-6-2011

Pain

When pain comes to live in the body
It has a way of taking over
my whole awareness,
making me feel trapped in my body with the pain.

But then there's the gratitude
for the love and concern of friends
who wish me well,
ask how I am,
some of them reaching out of their own pain
to touch me in healing.

And so my awareness moves
from the pain to my heart
opening in gratitude
for the gift of friends,
sending messages of concern.

A true friend is one who shares
pain and laughter
love and companionship
sorrow and joy.

I give thanks for friends.
I give thanks to friends:
manifestations of divine love.

8-6-2011
6.11 pm

Words of inclusive love

A prayer

Source of all life and love,
We give thanks for the beautiful diversity of love,
The glorious rainbow of sexuality,
and the myriad ways to give and receive love.
We give thanks for the love of lesbians, gays, heterosexuals, bisexuals, transgender,
chosen celibates, whose souls are aflame with *eros* and *agape*.
We give thanks for the love of friends, families, companion animals, mothers and
fathers, sisters and brothers, uncles and aunts and second cousins once removed.
We give thanks for the random acts of kindness shown by strangers to each other.
We give thanks for our beloved community.
May all these loves be strengthened and renewed
by wisdom, patience, tolerance, forbearance, forgiveness and courtesy.
May all these loves recognise and rejoice in each other
as part of the great tapestry of love.
May all beings be filled with loving-kindness,
and may justice roll down like waters
and righteousness like an ever-flowing stream.
Amen.

A Benediction

Let us embody the values of the rainbow flag of lesbian, gay, bisexual and transgender
people.
Red is the root of spirit, found in beloved community,
Orange is for *Eros*, the fire of spirit, the experience of erotic connection,
Yellow is for self-esteem, the strong core of spirit,
Green is for love, the heart of spirit, the verdant growth of the soul,
Blue is for self-expression, the voice of spirit, calling out for justice,
Purple is the eye of spirit, which sees inwardly with the eye of wisdom.
And all the colours together form the crown of spirit, the experience of spirituality.

(These could be used for a Bridge of Light celebration)

22-12-2010

Sometimes we do not hear the call

Sometimes we do not hear the call,
the still small voice that speaks to us
in the watches of the night.
Sometimes we do not recognise the messenger,
nor hear the message,
though reality patiently sends it over and over,
showing the way, opening the door.
O source of all wisdom,
help us to discern the subtle whispers
among the tumult of conflicting messages.
Help us to find the harmonious way
among the many branching possibilities.
Help us to recognise the messengers from the Divine
in their many forms.
Help us to hear the voice of love
calling us to community, to justice and to peace.
Amen.

17-11-2010

My christology

> "The incarnation is true, not of Christ exclusively, but of Man universally, and
> God everlastingly." - James Martineau

My christology is neither high nor low,
but broad and deep.

We are all Christ,
emerging wet and shining
from the River Jordan,
with the light of heaven
shining on us.

We are all Buddha,
reborn each moment,
arising dependent,
Buddha-nature unfolding.

We are all John Barleycorn,
cut down in autumn,
ploughed back into the earth each winter,
putting on green shoots in spring.

We are all Aradia,
bringing her subversive message of hope
to an oppressed people.

We are all messiahs,
and we must all save the world
together, like rainbow warriors.

Let us recognise the work
to which we are called,
and open our sacred hearts to the world.

2-7-11, 6.01 am

- Aradia is the messianic figure supposed to have appeared to Italian witches and taught
  them the mysteries of Diana
- Christology is what you think the nature of Christ is (in relation to God and humanity)
- John Barleycorn is a dying and resurrecting vegetation spirit in Wiccan mythology
- The Legend of the Rainbow Warriors is a prophecy of the coming of saviours

Grandfather God

Grandfather God,
who trails beards of moss over the rocks and the trees
and decks the bushes in autumn with hairy seed-cases;
you are not an authority figure but a playmate.
We come to your house on holy days
to play hide and seek,
sing lustily,
and have tea and cakes.
Your wisdom is of the humble variety,
quietly spoken, close to the earth.
You love to gaze at the stars
and give bread to the ducks.
You don't tell me off,
you just hold me close
and tell me jokes about life.
Tell us another story, Grandpa.
Tell us how we are loved.
Let me bring you something -
a cup of tea? a biscuit?
No. Only my heart will do,
as I sit cradled in your arms
by the hearth of dreams.
A heart bruised by experience,
brimming with joy,
suffused with love.
Well, then.
Cheerio, Grandpa.
See you soon.

8-9-2009

Prayers for the seasons

Harvest prayer

Weaver of all destiny, source of change, process of becoming,
You are the warp and weft of our lives,
The divinity in everything.
We see you reflected in the sunrise and the sunset,
The swelling ear of corn, the crop ready for harvest,
And the seed ready to begin the cycle again.
We see you in the cycles of history, the process of liberation,
The widening circle of compassion.
May we be part of the process of healing and reconciliation,
May our lives be a harvest of love and wisdom.
For it is written: "As you sow, so shall you reap":
May we sow harmony and joy, truth and love,
And reap the joys of beloved community,
Peace and justice, equality and inclusion.
Amen.

Samhain / All Hallows Prayer

O Source of all being
Mysterious Presence that guides us and shadows us
From whom we emerge and to whom we return
Help us to face the mystery of death
with grace and wisdom.
Help us to understand the cycles of life, death and birth,
honouring the sacrifices of those who suffered
to bring us freedom and knowledge.
Wise Crone and Ancient of Days,
You weave the mysterious patterns of life
And stand always at the well of destiny,
Beckoning us to the source of our being,
ever deeper, ever nearer to the dark swirling waters.
May we feel connected to the divinity
at the heart of all that is, and feel it in our deep heart's core.
May we know the satisfaction of a life well lived,
And sing the song that we have come to sing.
Amen.

Meditations

The sacred

I invite you to close your eyes, and to choose something – a place, a concept, an object, a person – that you regard as sacred. What is the quality in it that evokes the sacred for you? What values or virtues does it represent? Are they values or virtues that find an echo within you? Is the sacredness an inherent quality of it? Or does it shine through it, as if its source is elsewhere? Just focus for a while on your sacred place, concept, thing or person. Allow its virtue to shine for you; hear its inner music, smell its perfume. [long pause] Now let the place, concept, thing or person fade from your mind and just focus on the virtue itself, and recognise its reflection in your own heart.

Innovation

I invite you to close your eyes, and think of a time that you tried something new. Maybe the first time you rode a bike, or your first kiss, or the first time you tried a type of food that you were convinced you didn't like. Maybe it was the first time you tried a new spiritual practice: meditation, or visualisation, or prayer, or elaborate ritual. Maybe it was when you did something scary, like capsizing a canoe or doing a parachute jump.

Try to remember how it felt before you did it. Were you scared, resisting, apprehensive, hesitant? Was there someone there to help you get over your fear? What did they do? Were they supportive and kind, or did they push you into it – being "cruel to be kind"?

Try to remember how it felt while you were doing it. When did fear change to pleasure? If it did... What kind of pleasure was it? Quiet satisfaction or wild exhilaration?

Now try to remember how it felt afterwards. Did you want to do it again? Did it make you more willing to try new things? Did it change how you felt about yourself? [pause]

Hold the memory of these feelings in your mind. When you are ready, open your eyes and return to the present and your companions here.

The body

I invite you to take one breath for the earth beneath our feet, one for the sky above us, and one for the sea that surrounds us[1]. Be aware of your body, and release any tension in your feet ... legs ... belly ... chest ... arms ... neck ... and head. Now look within yourself – what images arise? ... [pause] ...The body contains darkness – the velvet darkness of the flesh, the nourishing darkness of the earth. The body contains water – water that answers to the call of the Moon, water that nourishes life. The body contains earth – the chalk-white bones that hold us up. The body contains air – the air that we breathe. The body contains fire – the spark of life, the warmth of the flesh, the pulse of the blood. And the body contains light – the spark of the Divine in every heart, the light of reason in every mind. The body holds our memories – memories of happiness and sadness, memories that make us who we are. The body gives rise to our dreams – dreams of freedom and peace, dreams of love and passion. The body holds our spirit, our consciousness, our inner life. The body fixes us in time and place, allowing us to experience the present moment in all its fullness. Let us be present now – present to our bodies, present to each other, present to this precious moment. [long pause] Let us be present now. [music]

The Divine

What is the Divine? Is it the still small voice that whispers to your conscience in the watches of the night? ... Is it love, that leaps like a spark from heart to heart? ... Is it inspiration, stirring the mind to insight and poetry? ... Is it power and glory and might? ... Or is it humility and integrity and wonder? ... Is it compassion, that pities the poor and friendless and alone? ... Is it the power of creativity, that continuously creates all existence? ... Is it the power that sustains the universe? ... Is it the source of all that is? ... Is it the beauty and grandeur of nature? ... Is it eternally one and the same, unchanging, ceaseless and beyond all thought? ... Is it constantly changing and evolving, growing like a tree into the vastness of time? ... Is it the void, the nothingness and silence beyond existence, where we can let our minds rest? ... It may be all or none of these things, but we feel its touch when we let our minds rest in the ultimate ground of our being, the silence and awe and wonder. Let us go within to our own silent contemplation of the Divine.

---

[1] Taking a breath for the earth, sky, and sea is borrowed from Druid meditations and visualisations

Love

We cannot define love, we do not know what it is, or how many kinds of love there are. We can only experience love.

Sometimes it is the love that dare not speak its name for fear of persecution. Sometimes love is tragic, as in the love of Oscar for Alfred, the love of David for Jonathan, the love of Eloise and Abelard. Sometimes love is fulfilled, as in the love of Ruth for Naomi, the love of Jesus and Mary Magdalene.

Sometimes love is fleeting and profligate, wounding us suddenly and painfully. There is Eros, erotic love; *Fili*, the love of children and parents; *Storge*, married love; and Agape, Divine love. There is *Ahava*, the love that gives, and *Chesed*, steadfast love. There is the love of friends, and the miracle of love for strangers, showing hospitality to others. There is the love that includes the broken and the wounded, and there is the wonderful gift of forgiveness, given and received. Let us ponder and treasure our own experiences of love. [pause for silent meditation]

Let us give thanks for the miracle of love.

Ancestors – a meditation for Samhain / All Souls

Take a deep breath. Be aware of your body, with all its genetic quirks – the shape of your face, ears and nose, the colour of your eyes, the texture of your hair, the shape of your body. All this is inherited from your biological ancestors. Think of what you know of your family history, and feel your connection to the generations that have gone before. And now reflect on all who have worshipped in this place over the generations – dissenters seeking freedom from imposed creeds, freedom to use their reason to interpret religious ideas, and tolerate the different ideas of others.

Who are our ancestors? Are they the people we are descended from genetically? Or are they the people who have inspired us, shown us the way to wisdom, freedom, love and enlightenment? Or both?

I invite you to think now of someone you find inspiring. It can be a mentor from your own life, or someone from history whom you find inspiring. What qualities or deeds of theirs do you celebrate and honour? How are these reflected in your own life? Spend some time reflecting on that person and what they mean to you.

Honouring the ancestors
Everyone who wishes to do so can come to the front, light a candle for a loved one who has died, and speak about them.

The web of being

As you sit in the silence of our beloved community, be aware of the connections of love and friendship that connect you with all those around you. Imagine that each of our hearts is a beacon lit in the night, a fire of hope and courage and love at which others can warm themselves. Sometimes we have failed to share our warmth. But many times we have made a difference to the lives of others by reaching out to them in love. See all the shining threads of love and care that connect you to others, and see the threads of love wound around the whole world, as we are all interconnected; a network of shining beacons of love embracing the world. {silence}

Let us always be mindful of the web of being that connects us all together.

The trees and the forest

As we sit in the quiet of the evening, breathing softly, each with our own particular concerns, let us be aware of our common humanity. Each of us has our own hidden wellspring of joy, our own experience of sorrow, our unique perspective on the Divine and its relationship with the world.

Let us celebrate the diversity of dreams and visions.

Think of the tress in the woods: each grows into its individual shape to fit its particular place and the events that have shaped its growth, but each is recognisable as one of a species: oak, birch, holly, maple, yew, beech, hawthorn.

Religions are like that too: each has its own unique characteristics, shaped by place, culture and history; but all of them have their roots in the fertile soil of human experience, and all seek the living waters of the divine presence.

Let us honour the beauty and diversity of religions in the world, whilst loving and cherishing our own particular visions and traditions, recognising that we too are rooted in our common humanity, all seeking the nourishment of the endless outpouring of love and wisdom that we call by many names, all of them holy.

Chalice lightings

As we light this transitory flame

As we light this transitory flame
May a perpetual flame burn in our hearts
As we lift up this earthen chalice
May our hearts be filled with living waters

We gather here within these walls

We gather here within these walls
Hallowed by the community
that has gathered here over the centuries.
Countless hands have tended the flame of fellowship
and countless more will keep the light burning.

As we light the chalice flame

As we light the chalice flame today
Let us not hide our light under a bushel
but be a beacon of hope to all around us.

The fullness of life's experiences

The chalice is the fullness of life's experiences
And the emptiness of innocent openness to wonder
As we light the chalice flame
Let us explore the empire of the senses,
Let us celebrate experience and experiment:
the twin expressions of freedom, reason and tolerance.

The flame rises from the chalice

The flame rises from the chalice
as prayer proceeds from the heart.
The flame spends itself in giving light
But the heart is never spent in prayer.
May our hearts be inflamed with love
for all that is.

Sharing the radiance

The flame consumes the wick,
Constantly changing and dancing
Sharing its radiance with us.
So may our souls be aflame with divine love
Sharing our radiance with others.

We see the flame rise up

As we light the chalice,
We see the flame rise up,
held in the bowl of the chalice.
Just so our spirits yearn for the Divine
Held in the circle of community.

It shines everywhere

The divine is everywhere,
Pervading all hearts,
All beings, all existence.
It shines everywhere.
The flame is a symbol of divine light
Available to all humanity,
Through all religions and all experience.
The chalice is a symbol of community,
The community of all beings.

Seasonal chalice lightings

Samhain / All Souls

(Christian festival of remembrance; Pagan festival of the start of winter, and of freedom)

 Many before us have sought the light of understanding
Heretics, witches, lovers of freedom
This chalice symbolises the communion of Jan Hus
and the lamp upon the altars of ancient Greece.
This flame represents the light of hope
kindled by the dreamers and visionaries of the past
which we must carry into the future.

Diwali

(Hindu festival of lights)

Our chalice flame is one light among a myriad
A myriad lights for the festival of lights
Floating upon the dark waters of the river
and illuminating the depths of winter.

Hanukkah

(Jewish festival of liberation from oppression)

As we recall the ancient miracle of Hanukkah
With its nine days of holy oil
So we kindle our own holy light
And hope that its light will continue to shine in our hearts.

Yule

(Pagan festival of winter solstice)

At the time when the day is shortest
And the Sun shows herself only briefly above the horizon
We light this flame of hope
To represent the solstice fire on the hilltop
That ancient people lit to remind the sun to return
And we honour the cycle of the seasons
As their tides are echoed in our own lives.

Christmas

(Christian festival of midwinter)

Every child is a miracle and a mystery
And in the one born at midnight
In the dark time of the year
We see all children leaping into the light
And as we light this flame
We honour the light in everyone,
the Christ in everyone,
the child in everyone.

Eid

(Muslim feast at the end of Ramadan)

The morning star is caught in the horns of the Moon;
the month of fasting is over.
Put on your robes of joy
and come to the feast.
Kindle the holy flame of love
and welcome joy.

Imbolc / Candlemas

**(Pagan festival of early spring & Brighid /
Christian festival of St Brighid & Purification of the Virgin)**

A crown of lights
For the gentle healer
A crown of lights
For the inspired poet
A crown of lights
For the smith of dreams
A crown of lights
For the midwife of Ireland
And the chalice of life
For her wisdom.

Spring Equinox

(Pagan festival)

Day and night are equal now
But day has the upper hand.
In the endless dance of dark and light
And the turning of the Wheel of the Year
A moment's pause at the equinox
to reflect on the glory of the dance.
As we light our chalice flame,
It recalls the fire of the Sun
dancing on the hills.

Palm Sunday

(Christian: Jesus' arrival in Jerusalem)

The cries of welcome for the anointed one
rang in the streets.
Each saw the fulfilment of their hopes and dreams.
May we know the fulfilment that is to be found
in our own spark of the Divine
in our own hearts
and as we light this chalice flame
let us remember all those who were raised up
only to be cast down
and be careful to worship only the highest and the deepest.

Holi

(Hindu and Sikh spring festival)

The many colours of the spring
Are splashed exuberantly over the land
And so people splash colour in imitation of nature.
May all the colours of the rainbow
Be contained in our chalice flame.

Tenebrae

(Christian observance of the night before the crucifixion)

The night seemed endless:
drawn like a veil over the suffering land
that cried out in its sleep,
"The Anointed One is betrayed."
The Sun was eclipsed, the veil of the temple rent in two
But a single star of hope
Illuminated the uncanny dark:
the resilience of the human spirit.
And so we light our chalice flame
in honour of the Divine spark in each one of us.

Easter

(Christian festival of resurrection)

Joy to the World
Life calls to life
Arise! Awake!
Fear no more the silence of the tomb
For the lives of humanity
are strung like pearls on the thread of the spirit[2]
and the pearl shines in the darkness of the deep.
Life arises,
Life unending,
Life triumphant!
Spirit like a flame catching on the wick of flesh.

Beltane

(Pagan festival of spring & love)

The trees are green, the forests awakened from the sleep of winter.
Deck the boughs with ribbons;
make bowers in the field for Robin and Marian.
Make merry; sing, dance, laugh and make love.
As the Beltane fires are kindled on the hilltops,
So we light our chalice flame,
in honour of the Spirit of Life,
ever resurgent, leaping and laughing.

---

[2] This line comes from Dion Fortune's novel, *The Sea Priestess*

Midsummer

(Pagan festival)

The light is at the height of its power
The Sun shines fiercely.
But now that power must wane
Descending into the darkness
to be reborn.
Light and darkness dance
in the crucible of desire
and bring forth life.
So we light the chalice flame
to represent life, hope, love and laughter.

Lammas / Lughnasadh

(Pagan festival of harvest)

The corn is gathered,
The last sheaf bound,
The harvest gathered in.
Life is given that life may continue.
Let the games begin.
Let it be a dance we do.
As each sheaf is safely gathered in
Let's illuminate the chalice flame
As we dance the harvest in.

Harvest

(Christian)

We reap the fields and orchards
We gather in the wheat.
The gleaners at the margins
Look for our gifts.
Share the bounty of the land:
Open heart and open hand.
As we light our chalice flame
So we laud the holy name
of love.

Rosh Hashanah

(Jewish festival of the creation of the world)

As the bird of space moved over the face of the waters
As the creative word was spoken
As the universe was born on this day
And life first emerged from the fertile clay
May the Divine Presence be with us
as we light this chalice:
a flame hovering over the void.

Printed in Great Britain
by Amazon.co.uk, Ltd.,
Marston Gate.